IN
F

GW00648842

By Gerald Haigh

Cartoons:
Phil Hailstone

Published by:

Teachers' Pocketbooks
Laurel House, Station Approach,
Alresford, Hampshire SO24 9JH, UK
Tel: +44 (0)1962 735573
Fax: +44 (0)1962 733637
E-mail: sales@teacherspocketbooks.co.uk
Website: www.teacherspocketbooks.co.uk

*Teachers' Pocketbooks is an imprint of
Management Pocketbooks Ltd.*

Series Consultant: **Brin Best**.

All rights reserved. No part of this publication
may be reproduced, stored in a retrieval
system or transmitted in any form, or by any
means, electronic, mechanical, photocopying,
recording or otherwise, without the prior
permission of the publishers.

© Gerald Haigh 2007.

This edition published 2007.

ISBN 978 1 903776 78 0

British Library Cataloguing-in-Publication
Data – A catalogue record for this book is
available from the British Library.

Design, typesetting and graphics by **Efex Ltd**.
Printed in UK.

Contents

Foreword

It's disappointing to be turned down for a job, but doubly so when you feel you've let yourself down. As you went over the selection hurdles you never really hit your stride. Perhaps you didn't even get an interview; perhaps you did get an interview, but didn't get the job. You may be asking yourself where you went wrong.

Or you may be attaching some blame to the selection committee for not drawing out the best in you. In UK schools, we have no tradition of employing professional recruiters whose specific job is to identify talent. Those who read our applications and interview us include governors, who may or may not have some recruitment training, together with headteachers and authority advisers whose considerable professional skills aren't always directly relevant to the immediate task.

This makes it even more important for ambitious and able teachers to take some control and be **adept at presenting** their **skills, attitudes and intentions** in the best possible light, **in writing and in face-to-face interviews**.

That's where this book comes in. Whether you're looking for your first teaching post or seeking to move to a new one, it won't necessarily guarantee you that ideal job, but it may well position you further up the grid for the start of the race.

Starting Out and Moving On ◀

 Job Seeking

 Gathering Information

 Writing the Application

 Preparing for Interview

 Interview Day

 The Interview

 It's All Over

Starting Out and Moving On

Teaching happens everywhere

Wherever there's human settlement there are children to be taught. That gives you the freedom to build your career in your way – near to home, in a new part of the UK, or abroad.

Within limits you can carve out the career that suits you: a ladder leading to headship and beyond, or a series of interesting parallel jobs that broaden your experience of life.

The key to satisfaction lies in knowing who you are and what you want, and then in making the choices that suit.

A career plan

Most people have a career plan, even if they don't admit it, or haven't articulated it clearly. Sometimes it's more a set of attitudes than a campaign blueprint. If you:

- Look at a successful teacher and think, *'I could do that'*
- Look at a headteacher and think, *'But I never want to do that'*
- Look at your bank balance and think, *'I could get by on three days a week'*
- Look at Africa and think, *'Those children need me'*

then you already have an embryo career plan. Recognise it, talk about it, think it through. But don't fill in too much detail, because it can all change. Hobbies, relationships, health can all play havoc with plans that are too closely written.

So, be prepared for changes of direction but throughout your career, from beginner to experienced head, pay attention to your professional development, adding appropriate qualifications wherever you can.

See yourself in context

If you're ambitious, wanting a career rather than just a job, it's important from the word go to be aware of where you are, in professional terms, compared with others. So from the moment you start applying for your first job, look around at the people who are doing the same – friends, fellow students, colleagues – and take notice of:

- Their levels of qualification
- The breadth and length of their previous experience
- The range, and types of responsibilities they can talk about

With this knowledge in mind, observe who's successful in the job market. Learn what's possible and realistic, what seems to work, what combination of attributes does the trick. Try to place yourself against the bigger teaching background; that way you'll develop realistic targets and aspirations. Do this to learn, not to score points.

Applaud others' success. Learn from them. Be inspired, not envious.

Your first post

It's not unusual for a student teacher to be offered a job in their teaching practice school. Often, the opportunity to continue working there cuts a swathe through a host of prior assumptions and plans. Here are the questions to ask yourself, and to discuss with your friends and tutors:

- Should you feel flattered? (Probably, though much depends on how desperate the school is for someone with your specialism)

- Do you really want to stay in the area? (Weigh this one up very carefully – living costs, family issues, quality of life)

- Is the school a good career launch pad? (This is complicated, and calls for a lot of thought)

- Is the job really what you want – specialism, age group, working environment? (If not, don't be afraid to say no and look further afield)

- Are you thinking, *'It'll do till something else turns up'* ? (If so, it's probably wrong to take it)

Judging when to move on

From the moment you start in teaching, to the end of your career, you'll always be thinking of the next job. Sometimes it'll just be in the back of your mind – but it will always be there, and will push its way forward as time goes on.

But when is the right time to move on? The easy answer is, *'When you feel it in your bones'* – and you do develop a sense of when it's time to go. Here's a teacher in her late thirties:

> *I was on the senior leadership team, just got my National Professional Qualification for Headship. The head was leaving, the deputy was definitely going to stay where she was. I gave a much praised speech at the head's retirement do, feeling confident on the stage before all the invited guests. When I walked back to my table with applause and nods and smiles all around, I suddenly realised I'd outgrown the role I was in and I knew I had to start the very next day looking at deputy headships.*

Judging when to move on

If it's not enough to depend on that feeling in the bones, here are some more specific pointers:

- You are qualified, experienced and competent to do a job one or more levels higher than where you are
- There's no obvious opening coming in your present school
- Even if there is, you aren't convinced that you want to work with the current team
- Your family life offers a window of opportunity – your partner's about to change jobs, you want a house move, your children are about to change schools

Leaving your first job

Leaving your first job is always one of the most difficult moves.
It's difficult because:

- If you have any moral principles at all, you feel
loyalty to the people who invested time and
resources in your early development (Even if
you had a bad time, and felt ill-treated, there
are always individuals to whom you feel
some obligation)

- Like a child leaving the nest, you're
leaving the only home you know

- You know little of other schools and
other jobs, and you dread making a
serious mistake. You know you'll be
expected to stay long enough in
your second job for your career to
develop, and you have to make
the right choice

Leaving your first job

Definitely complete your first year. If you leave during your first year it might be assumed that:

- You were unhappy at the school
- The problems were probably of your own making

Only if you can really see no alternative way of keeping your sanity and self-respect should you leave during your first year.

Try to do the second year too, and repay some of the investment in you.

Then you can go with a relatively clear conscience. In fact if you're obviously able and ambitious, the school will almost expect you to go at the end of your second year – or at least they won't be surprised.

Or maybe staying put

By the end of the second year you may consider that your career within the school is going to develop. The signs are:

- Your appraisals are excellent
- You're being given more responsibility
- You've successfully led some important projects
- You're being offered training and development opportunities
- Senior and middle leaders are looking for promotion, and jobs are opening up

Now's the time for a frank talk about your prospects with senior management. If it's a good school they'll offer you good advice:

'We'd be happy if you'd stay. We like your work. We're prepared to invest in your professional development, and – no promises mind – there'll be opportunities.'

'You're clearly going places. We can't see anything here for you any time soon, but we'll wholeheartedly support you if you want to go for promotion elsewhere.'

Be positive

Always, whatever career stage you're at – looking for your first job, going for promotion, aspiring to headship – move for a positive reason and to a job you really want. Any job you're going to chase seriously should live up to most of these conditions:

- It makes you keen to get started – because there's a definite challenge, but one that you feel equipped for
- It's in a school that's observably efficient and orderly
- It puts you among staff who seem relaxed, at ease with each other and with their work, ready to support keen newcomers
- It puts you with students you can connect with, who you feel need you, and who in time will respond to the way you work

There are others, but these are the basics. It won't have escaped your notice that they're very much linked; if one's there, it's likely that so are the others.

Gunners and doers

This is nothing to do with the Royal Artillery. It's about people who are always 'gunner' do something, but never do. Don't be a 'gunner'. Be a doer. Ask yourself two questions:

- Is there a role you've always fancied, and bored everyone's pants off about, which is probably within your reach?
- In the last twelve months have you made the slightest attempt to do anything about it?

If you've answered *'yes'* then *'no'*, face it, you're a gunner. Why are you a gunner? Because you're in the comfort zone; you know your way around; it's too much of an effort to move. **Don't be complacent.** In time, inevitably, your life will change around you. If you're in training your course will end; if you're in a school, you'll find it's in a permanent stage of change. The comfort zone *will* disappear.

Starting Out and
Moving On

 Job Seeking

 Gathering
Information

 Writing the
Application

 Preparing for
Interview

 Interview Day

 The Interview

 It's All Over

Job Seeking

How it works – the process

The teaching job market usually works like this:

1 A vacancy is identified and defined by the school or by the authority or organisation that runs the school. It may be a new post, a replacement, or a combination of both, eg a new post that includes the duties of an earlier one.

2 The post is advertised. The advertisement is carefully drawn up to attract the most suitable candidates, who are invited to write, phone or call for further details.

3 An application pack is sent out and applications awaited.

4 After the closing date for applications, representatives of the school and the employing organisation (local authority, trustees, company) select those to be interviewed.

5 Interviews are held and an appointment is made.

There are variations, but the basic and honest principle of open advertisement and competitive application and interview holds good for most teaching posts.

How it works – internal or external?

If a teacher with responsibility leaves a school, the post may well be filled internally. This will be because:

- There are excellent people working in the school, well known to management and there seems no advantage in looking elsewhere
- The school budget requires a staffing reduction
- Promoting a person internally creates a cheaper vacancy further down the hierarchy, perhaps for a newly qualified teacher

Unless the vacant promoted post is to be filled temporarily on an 'acting' basis, it must be advertised within the school and the correct appointment procedure followed. If the governors want a wider selection of applicants, and there's money for a new recruit at that level, they may advertise to outside candidates as well as internally.

Finding vacancies

Reading lots of ads gives you a better knowledge of the market. Study the job vacancies in the TES, Education Guardian, the local papers and on the internet. (Google various options: 'Teaching jobs', 'Teaching posts' and 'Education jobs' to make sure you don't miss anything.)

- Read beyond your preferred region, school type, salary level or subject. You may spot your ideal job in a section you hadn't considered
- Start a comparison chart of jobs broadly in line with what you're looking for – job title, school type, school size, area, salary range, closing date. (TES jobs website offers a personal online folder)
- Don't miss key points often at the top of the ad, eg is it a faith school?
- If it says what sort of person's required, look beyond the *'enthusiastic, committed'* clichés for clues as to the qualities and attitudes being sought

Send for the details

The moment you send for details you are under scrutiny. So make your email or letter professional and accurate. (It's not as difficult as you might imagine to misspell the name of the school, for instance. Guess how often the head of one C of E school in Warwickshire sees two errors in the three words 'Canon Maggs School'.)

When the details arrive, turn straight to the closing date for applications and write it on your calendar. If it's different from the date given on the advert or at all ambiguous, phone to clarify. The best application is useless if it's too late.

Expect to receive quite a sheaf of stuff in your application pack, including **a job specification, a person specification** and **details of the school**. Also, probably, some information about the authority and a statement about equal opportunities.

If you decide to apply, put the details and the form in a labelled folder with the closing date in bold on the front. Photocopy everything and put two copies away safely.

Job description and person specificaton

The **job description** is just what it says – a summary of the duties and responsibilities of the person doing the job.

If the job you're looking at isn't a straightforward permanent full-time job, eg if it's temporary or part-time or both, be clear about what sort of contract is being offered. If possible ask via a letter or an email so that you get a written reply. If you have any doubts about it, ask your professional association for advice.

The **person specification** is the key document. See it as a homing beacon leading you to the job. It sets out, in detail, what the person appointed to the job needs to have by way of qualifications, knowledge and experience. It's carefully written with a view to being non-discriminatory: an applicant either fits the specification or not.

It's also designed to be helpful to you, because it gives you the opportunity to show how you can match each of the set requirements.

Keep both documents to hand to guide you as you write your letter and prepare for interview.

Telling your school

If you're already in a teaching job, applying for another, you face the decision of when to tell the headteacher that you're planning to go.

Some people are embarrassed about this. There's no need to be. Remember:

- You aren't the centre of the universe
- Over the years every head sees maybe hundreds of teachers come and go
- The earlier your managers know you might be leaving, the better
- If you're ambitious and excellent, people expect you to move on
- Is it possible they're relieved you're going?
- You need a reference from your current head anyway, and it's discourteous not to ask first

So, the best advice is to tell the head as soon as you start to look. If you can't bring yourself to do that, then definitely speak up when you've decided to apply; you need to ask for permission to give the head as a reference. (See page 41.)

Giving notice

Teachers usually start new jobs at the beginning of a term – September, January, or after Easter.

If you're already in a teaching job, there are fixed dates by which you have to give notice. These will be defined in your contract of employment.

When you start serious job hunting, check these dates. If you can't find them, phone your HR department at the local authority and get the current dates as they affect you, in your present post. Don't accept guesses and folklore from the staffroom.

Occasionally your new school may want you to start earlier than your period of notice allows. The new school would have to approach your present school. They don't have to agree, and they may not.

Moving in the same school

If you apply for a job in your own school, whether it's internally or externally advertised, you may well be in competition with your own colleagues. How do you handle this?

Go through the process – application, interview, dress, conduct – exactly as you would if you were applying to another school. Even take the tour of the school if you're given the option. There'll be individuals involved in the decision who do not know you, and others who only know you a little and may be influenced by a casual impression. It's really important that you make a full and persuasive application that will stand up beside the ones from outside.

However, if you're an internal candidate for an externally advertised job you can't expect (contrary to oft-stated myth) an automatic interview 'for the experience'. Good practice requires that each candidate, internal and external, be treated even-handedly.

Chicken counting

Do not count your chickens. This applies to every job application but particularly to internal ones. It means two things:

❶ Even if you're urged to apply, or given strong hints or assurances that the job is virtually yours, make no plans or assumptions. It is quite possible for someone from outside to impress the panel enough to turn things around. And you will have absolutely no cause for complaint.

❷ Conversely, if you make what you think is a forlorn hope application (*'Oh blow it. I might as well have a go.'*) don't assume failure. None of those being interviewed (you included) is a no-hoper on paper. The reasoning that goes against the shoo-in candidate is equally capable of working on behalf of the outsider.

Keep in mind also that while governors take notice of their headteacher and local authority, they are often the ones who make the decision, and they may well feel they need to take a different view. After all, the head may not be there much longer.

Starting Out and Moving On

 Job Seeking

 Gathering Information

 Writing the Application

 Preparing for Interview

 Interview Day

 The Interview

 It's All Over

Gathering Information

Knowledge is the key

To convince the recruiters, you need to know as much as possible about both the school and the job, so study the application pack. As well as giving information, it gives implicit hints and prompts for your application and – you hope – interview.

- Use a highlighter pen to pick up significant facts and requirements
- Notice particularly anything that's mentioned as special to the school, or something the school is evidently proud of, eg a particular subject specialisation, a special unit for children with sensory impairment, a listed building, a reputation for drama or music, etc
- Study the school prospectus. It will give you further insight into the school's particular character

Next, if there's no general invitation, phone and arrange to visit the school (see page 45). This visit is ahead of, and entirely separate from, the 'official' visit that you'll be invited to make if you're selected for interview. The same rules apply though.

Get help

Recruit as much help as you can. So, for example, photocopy the details and the form and give them to trusted friends, colleagues and family to read. If you are already in a teaching post, ask a more experienced colleague or mentor to read the details. Ask them to highlight what they think are the key words and phrases, and to have a session with you talking through the main points. However:

Don't invite friends round for wine and a chat about the application. It'll lead to a confusion of ideas and pseudo-expertise backed up by anecdotes of dubious authenticity.

Do keep your head and be prepared to back your own judgement. Consulting others means just that. You listen, quietly ponder, and then use your own judgement.

Do the research

When you've studied the application pack, look further afield:

* Read the last Ofsted report online
* Look at published league table data
* Explore the school website
* Search the local newspaper's website for articles about the school

Interpret your research, eg what was the date of that last Ofsted report? Has the head changed since? And beware of making unwarranted correlations, eg between league tables and whether a school is a good place to work.

If there's anything still unclear, feel free to phone the school and ask for clarification. At any point in the job application process asking valid questions is permissible. Sensible questions and requests for further information, clearly and courteously put, present you as a serious candidate, genuinely interested in the school and the job.

Starting Out and Moving On

 Job Seeking

 Gathering Information

 Writing the Application

 Preparing for Interview

 Interview Day

 The Interview

 It's All Over

Writing the Application

Aims

As you write your application be clear about why you're doing it. Your aims are to get an interview and to get the panel feeling positive about you before they meet you.

1 You won't get the job if you're not interviewed. That means selling yourself hard on the application. Beware of thinking – *'I needn't put that in. I'll leave it for the interview.'* Many applicants do exactly that, thus risking ever having the chance to get the information across.

2 A good application actually biases the panel. They brighten up at the very thought of meeting you. You're ahead on points from the start.

Remember, you aren't trying to convince the recruiters that you're a wonderful person, rather that you're the right person for their job.

It's not about YOU; it's about THEIR job and whether YOU can do it.

Form, letter and CV

There's always a two-part process. You fill in a form and you write a letter of application. The two are complementary. Sometimes there's a CV as well.

Complete the form first. It focuses you on the shape of your career to date, filling in the gaps, reminding you of the various things you've done. Avoid unnecessary detail:

- **List all your jobs by title**. If there was responsibility, say so in one line
- **List your qualifications**. Usually the title is enough
- If you've been on lots of **training or courses**, no need to list them all, just recent ones that relate to the job you're applying for
- **Avoid jargon**. Governors hate it, heads have seen too much of it, and experience shows a high proportion of candidates misspell or misuse it!

Do at least one draft, on a photocopy of the original, with an eraser to hand. Your final copy should be in black (for photocopying). Above all, it must be factually accurate. Don't be tempted to upgrade your degree, enhance a job title or disguise career gaps. The following story about a teacher who did just that is true.

Be honest

A teacher with several jobs behind him applied for departmental headships without success. He became convinced that the problem lay in an episode a couple of years earlier when he'd left a new job after less than a term, feeling he'd made the wrong career choice. Deeply unhappy, he'd cut his losses and left in a cloud of ill-feeling. This very short stay stood out on his list of jobs, and drew persistent questions from interviewers.

So, after several failed applications, he wrote one simply leaving the problem job out and stretching the post before it to fill the gap. This time he was successful in landing a headship of department.

Within a month of taking up his new post, the authority's HR department, tracking back his record for pay purposes, uncovered his deception and he was sacked.

Harsh? Perhaps, but it did happen.

The letter

Your application letter should be neatly typed (unless handwriting is specified) in black on good quality white A4 paper. Two pages are more than enough. Don't run to a third.

- Use subheadings and bullet points. Remember it'll be read, along with numerous others, by people pressed for time, so make the job as easy as you can

- Use the person specification and the job description. Keep them by you. Use them to guide your headings and sections

- Provide evidence for your assertions. So rather than just saying you believe in a certain teaching method, give examples of how you've used it

Warning!

A lot of sharing of application letters goes on. It's well meaning and mutually supportive. But it has led to a head posting this entry on a teaching forum website:

> *I have just read two applications containing identical paragraphs...It had to happen one day with all these kind people sharing personal statements, application letters, presentations. The trouble is it now seems to devalue both applications...*

He then gives this advice:

> *Look at others' applications for inspiration only, then put them aside and write your own. Otherwise it could be the quickest ever route to the reject pile.*

Target your letter

It's a fundamental rule that every application should be individually prepared and targeted. Giving the reader the impression that you've fired off the same letter in different directions is a sure turn off. Here are some of the 'scattergun' mistakes that heads commonly see:

- Beginning *'Dear Sir or Madam.'* It takes just a phone call to discover the name
- Wrong school name. Unbelievable but very common
- No awareness of, or response to, the nature of the school or the area. A letter to an 80-pupil village school will be different from that to a big urban primary
- Wrong job. You've applied for KS1 and the job's in KS2
- You've mixed up your applications. This happens too. It's just lack of concentration
- Applying to the same school for two widely different vacancies. You think you're hedging your bets; the school thinks you can't make up your mind

Housekeeping errors

As well as mistakes of content, there are common 'housekeeping' errors. These can arise from tiredness, laziness or simple unawareness of what's acceptable:

- Not sticking to advice on length. If it says two sides, that's what it means – writing twice as much and then shrinking the font isn't advisable!
- Not understanding *'most recent first'* for your lists of jobs and qualifications
- Leaving some of the form blank. There's always something to write
- Writing *'see my letter'* or *'see my CV.'* The readers of the forms want to compare like with like without leafing through other papers
- Untidy form with crossings out or tea stains. (You didn't make a practice copy did you?)
- Poor spelling, grammar and punctuation. If you have weaknesses in these areas, get your practice copy carefully checked by someone who doesn't

The curriculum vitae (CV)

A CV is a permanently existing, but continuously updated, summary of your experience and qualifications, intended for whoever requires it. It doesn't replace the application form or the letter, either or both of which will probably duplicate much of your CV.

The business world places great emphasis on the CV. It's less like that in teaching, where a good application form and effective, targeted letter are what count. Only send a CV if they ask for it. It should be:

- Extremely **neat** and not over-egged with layout tricks
- Absolutely **accurate** in content and in presentation
- **Relevant** – with the emphasis on more recent work and qualifications
- **Balanced** – that's to say the eye should fall on what's important, so start with recent qualifications and work back. Do the same when listing your jobs
- **Detailed** – don't just give job titles, add a brief summary of your responsibilities
- **Honest** about any gaps in your employment record

References

The application form will ask for two, maybe three, referees. In many areas of working life, references are taken up after the job offer, which is 'subject to satisfactory references'. Teaching is different in that the offer is usually made on the day of the interview, which means references are usually in before that.

Website chat among teachers shows lots of misunderstanding of the practice around references:

> *'I sent out the application form and they rang the school for a reference the morning they got the form, just as I was going to tell the Head.'*

This is a teacher who didn't know that you ask potential referees *before you post the application* if you may give their details. This isn't a formality. Referees have been known to refuse, and it's their right to do so.

Who do you ask to be referees?

If you're already teaching in a school, you must give your current head as the main referee. There's no really acceptable reason for not doing so. If you don't, it raises questions and the panel may contact your head anyway.

It can be difficult to find a second referee, and almost impossible to find a third.

There's not usually much point in giving your immediate line manager because your head will probably ask them for information anyway. Try:

- The head of a previous school if it's not too long ago
- Teaching practice school if it's recent
- Youth workers, sports managers where you've given your time

For the third reference, you may have to resort to a character reference from a family friend in good standing, (eg vicar or other religious leader, magistrate) who can write from a private address and just say you're honest and a pillar of society.

When the reference is used and how

Often, only the references of short-listed candidates are taken up but if there are just a few applications, everybody's might be taken up. Conversely, if there are lots of applications, references will be taken up for promising candidates – 'the long list'.

The weight given to references varies according to the interviewing panel:

> *'I worked with a chair of governors who openly said that references weren't worth the paper they were written on. That's extreme, but what I will say is that references are rarely as important as candidates think they are.'*
>
> ### Headteacher

A panel already thinking of appointing a candidate will feel supported by an excellent reference – and a wavering member might be convinced by it. However, a reference rarely changes a panel's mind completely – unless it reveals a dishonest application.

Starting Out and
Moving On

 Job Seeking

 Gathering
Information

 Writing the
Application

 Preparing for
Interview

 Interview Day

 The Interview

 It's All Over

Preparing for Interview

You're called for interview

Ideally you'll receive a letter inviting you for interview, but if the school needs to get on with the process, it might be a phone call giving quite short notice.

Accept promptly. The selection committee want to be sure they have a viable number of candidates committed to attending.

You can obviously withdraw between accepting and attending, either because you've changed your mind or because you've got another job. But do it as soon as you know. Be courteous and tell them why. It does no harm to leave a good impression.

Check your travelling arrangements. If it's at all possible, do a test run to the school – you'll want to look round the area anyway.

Visiting the school

Don't be afraid to ask about a visit. A preliminary visit is a must, even if it's a brand new unopened school. You can see the site and walk the neighbouring streets.

Try to visit on a working day, separate from the interview. Do this even if a look round the school is available on the interview day. The purpose of your visit is:

* To confirm that the school is well run with good discipline and purposeful learning
* To clarify any uncertainties about the job itself – what it entails, where it sits in the school organisation
* To check out the area; to see where you might live should you have to move home
* To let people in the school have a look at you. If you don't visit and others do, you're at a disadvantage

On your school visit

Keep eyes and ears open. Watch and listen for:

- Rowdy classrooms. Any school can have the odd one, but most classrooms should look and sound purposeful and orderly
- Wandering children. In lesson time corridors should be quiet. If you're with any member of staff, teacher or not, they should be checking any child found on the loose
- Traffic between lessons. Children should be orderly and self-controlled, and certainly not intimidating to a visitor
- Children you meet in corridors and shared areas. They should be politely relaxed and smiling. (Sneering, whispered remarks, insolent stares are not good signals of the school's health)
- Litter. Some schools have a blind spot for litter that looks terrible to a visitor

Staff welfare

A good sign of the attitude to staff is to judge whether it's 'Staffroom Heaven' or 'Staffroom Hell.'

In 'Staffroom Heaven', the staffroom is:

- Spacious, clean and tidy
- Free of clutter, outdated papers, piles of books
- Comfortable, with good quality furniture
- Divided into work and sitting areas or separate rooms
- Well equipped with kitchen facilities, in a clearly defined area
- Provided with the means to make good quality hot drinks
- Staffed by a neat and efficient person serving break-time drinks and snacks

All of this says, *'We value our colleagues, and repay their commitment by giving them excellent break facilities.'*

Staff welfare

In 'Staffroom Hell', the staffroom is:

- Housed in an inadequate and inaccessible room
- Badly furnished with items unwanted somewhere else
- Untidy, with piles of paper, dirty crocks and half-eaten lunches around
- Not divided between work and leisure
- Provided with inadequate self-service kitchen and drinks facilities

All of this says, *'We no longer notice the state of our facilities and don't even hesitate to ask visitors to use them.'*

Asking questions

During your school visit, as well as looking and listening, ask questions.

Go away feeling as certain as you can be of:

- The exact demands of the job
- Its place in the hierarchy and the salary structure
- The rooms you'll be working in
- What your office is like (if it's that kind of job)
- What admin/technical support will be available to you
- What the teaching load is likely to be

Presenting yourself

Any and every time people in the school meet you, they're adding to their overall impression of you. So:

- **Be punctual.** Allow plenty of time and then add some more. Parking is often difficult, and in some schools you can lose ten minutes tracking down the main entrance
- **Dress smartly.** As you would for business
- **Be well mannered.** Offer handshakes, smile, make confident eye-contact, give full attention to whoever's speaking
- **Treat everyone equally.** Not only is it simple courtesy, you also just don't know what influence any individual has over your appointment
- **Be attentive and warm to the pupils.** They quickly spot candidates who are patronising or insincere

Post-visit homework

After the preliminary visit, sit down and do an audit of your professional skills.

Add examples of how you've demonstrated them in your work. Go through again, considering how these skills and examples line up with the requirements of the job you're going for.

This process alone will arm you for many interview questions, particularly for the one that says, *'Can you give us an example of that?'*

Guard against going blank at the interview by studying what you've written. Perhaps tape copies up around your home. Mentally (or out loud if you like, perhaps while driving) rehearse answers to the most obvious questions.

Keep remembering, as you did when writing the application: It's not about YOU. It's about THEIR job and whether YOU can do it.

Focus on what you can offer

Take some time to focus yourself on two areas.

1. Your personal qualities, eg:

- 'I'm confident and successful in the classroom.'
- 'I get on well with colleagues.'
- 'I am supportive and sympathetic to less experienced colleagues.'
- 'I am respected by parents and colleagues.'
- 'I enjoy the company of children.'
- 'I am professional, diligent and honest.'
- 'I have skills that I know other people do not have.'

2. The key messages that say you can do the job, eg:

- 'I have experience in the area you're looking for.'
- 'I have the right qualifications.'
- 'I'm accustomed to working in the kind of team you have in mind.'
- 'I have the required subject knowledge and classroom skills.'
- 'I have made good progress so far, and aim to continue.'

Notch up your professional knowledge

You now know some of the challenges of the new job. Write them down.
Next, read as much as you can about the latest thinking. As you do so, make
notes directly related to the challenges you've written down.

- Read the education supplements such as TES and Guardian Education thoroughly.
  Study their websites and search them for articles relevant to your application and
  your area of specialisation
- Study the specialist websites (see page 110)
- Browse 'Amazon' for books (then find them in your library if you can't afford to
  buy them)
- Immediately before your interview, watch out for media announcements which you
  can use to show that you're alert to what's going on in education

But don't trot out information just for the sake of it. It has to be relevant to the job
you're applying for.

Portfolio

Not everyone keeps a work portfolio, but it's common for teaching jobs other than senior management – and they sometimes appear there too. It should contain:

* Examples of your planning and assessment
* Photographs of pupils' work and events you've organised
* Examples of children's work in key curriculum areas
* Professional development evidence – coursework, appraisals, lesson observations

Build your portfolio up over time, selecting and rejecting as better material comes to hand. Keep it in a very presentable but simple A3 folder, not one with lots of pockets from which it's difficult to extract items quickly!

Before you go to an interview, go through your portfolio and have in it only items that are relevant to the job you're going for. Keep copies of everything so that you can offer to leave your portfolio with the interview panel.

The interview lesson

The letter inviting you for interview may well inform you that you'll be required to teach a demonstration lesson. Don't worry: all the candidates will be in the same position. Again, knowledge is the key. Find out:

- What you'll have to teach
- The length of the session
- How it fits into the normal scheme of work, especially what came before
- Nature of the group – number, age, ability
- Children with special needs (including gifted and talented)
- The discipline and reward policy as you're able to apply it
- Available resources
- Other adults you're expected to involve, eg TA, SEN assistant

The interview lesson

Even if the time you're given is artificially short, prepare **a three-part lesson**: starter, main activity, plenary.

Select a **lesson aim** that you'll be able to express in one sentence on the board at the beginning.

If the subject's appropriate (and with imagination most are), consider a short section of **role play or drama**, to show that you aren't fixated on written work.

Risky or safe?

Do you prepare a 'risky' lesson, eg one that involves the children in a lot of movement/noise – or do you play safe? It's always a judgement call, based on your feeling after visiting the school and meeting the people.

Pros

Some heads will admire a spectacular lesson that works.

Some heads are seeking creativity and new ideas.

Cons

The lesson can fall apart (after all, you don't know the children).

Some heads would rather see you in action on bread and butter stuff.

Resources

Whichever kind of lesson you opt for:

- Be prepared to take in your own basic items – spare pens, marker pens, paper, whatever the children are likely to ask for
- Don't plan a lesson that relies on too much ICT unless you're specifically asked to – too much can go wrong. Whatever equipment you use, prepare and test it in advance – and be ready for it still going wrong. Prepare for a power cut
- Prepare good, professional looking support resources on big sheets of paper – key words, pictures, graphs. Either use them from the start, or have them to hand if the ICT doesn't work
- Prepare differentiated tasks to include the range of abilities
- If it's in a science lab or D & T room, make a note to befriend the technician – he/she can make all the difference for you

Starting Out and Moving On

 Job Seeking

 Gathering Information

 Writing the Application

 Preparing for Interview

 Interview Day

 The Interview

 It's All Over

Interview Day

What to wear

Dress really is important. Don't try to convince yourself, *'If they really want me they'll take me as I am.'* It won't work. Remember you're dealing with lay governors as well as professionals. Dress for business: conservatively, modestly, thoughtfully and extremely well.

- Clothes perfectly clean and pressed
- Shirt or blouse immaculate and crisp
- Hair neat and well cared for
- Jewellery minimal but tasteful
- Shoes in good repair and well polished

Take advice from several trusted people. If necessary, beg and borrow the gear but make sure it fits comfortably. If undecided, always lean to the conservative.

If you look the part, you'll feel right

What not to wear

Do you need to be told to avoid the following?

- Trainers, flip flops. Many people lose the plot beyond the bottom of their trousers. It will be noticed
- Loud or joky ties. In dubious taste, even among friends, and totally unacceptable in an interview
- Revealing garments. They don't impress. People will comment privately, but they're not saying what you think they're saying
- Shirt with no collar (male). No tie is just OK. No collar is a step too far

Attitude and behaviour no-no's

You know the first impression is important so what can push you backwards beyond the start line?

Slouching. Hands in pockets, shoulders hunched says, *'I don't care'*.

Poor handshake. Be firm but not over-enthusiastic.

Body odour/halitosis. All you can do is ask your best friend for frankness, then nip to the loo for last minute deodorising, gargling, whatever works.

Chewing gum. Possibly de rigueur if you're seeking to manage a football club, but not for a teaching job.

iPod. Seen occasionally (and unbelievably) on some student interviewees. Don't bring one into the building at all.

Being **opinionated and loud** on the tour of the school.

Taking a **mobile phone** call. Switch off (not to silent) before you pass the front door.

Show courtesy

Everything we've said about the school visit applies also to the interview day but more so.

Turn up. Sounds obvious, but if you're withdrawing, let them know. A reputation for discourtesy can follow you.

Be on time. That means not too early as well as not too late. Too early can be embarrassing if they don't know what to do with you.

Behave well in the waiting area if you're all in the school together with other candidates. Yes, you're nervous, but don't let that draw you into nervy gossiping or feeble jokes. Keep quiet. It does no harm to come across as a dark horse.

Internal candidate

It's very common to find that there's an internal candidate being interviewed. You may be courteously told this, or you may not. There are stories of the internal candidate being brought, dishevelled, from the classroom and ushered in for a rapid interview.

Don't panic. Even a favoured internal candidate can lose the job at the interview.

Forget the internal candidate. Forget all the other candidates. Concentrate on interviewing as strongly as you possibly can.

It's not over till it's over.

The Interview

How does it work?

Interview arrangements vary considerably. Here's just one way:

1 All the candidates (typically three, four or five) arrive in the morning and tour the school.

2 Each candidate teaches a lesson and also makes a presentation to the panel.

3 All the candidates have lunch, perhaps with staff or pupils.

4 The candidates are based in a waiting room/the staffroom, and called in turn for interview. They either then leave, to be phoned later, or return to the waiting room.

5 After the last interview, the panel discuss their decision.

6 The successful candidate is offered the job, either on the phone or back in the interview room. The others receive a word of encouragement and perhaps the offer of a formal debrief.

Other possibilities include an in-tray exercise for management posts, and – for senior posts – the two-stage 'knockout', where the first interviews result in a shortlist for second interviews.

What are panel members looking for?

Clearly the interview is intended to show the panel who the best person is for the advertised job. However, each panel member also has a subsidiary agenda:

The parent governor: *'Can I see this person teaching my child?'*

'Of course each child is individual and has individual strengths, weaknesses and needs. Appreciating this and building understanding by listening and by involving parents/carers is an important part of the job for me.'

Head (or department head): *'How will this person fit in with my carefully built team?'*

'I've always enjoyed working with my colleagues, sharing strengths and learning from each other.'

Local authority inspector: *'Is this someone who can help address some of our concerns about this school?'*

'For me, the whole purpose of our work is to improve the children's learning.'

Do you want the job?

Even as you wait to be called for interview you need to be clear that you want this job. You have much more information about the school than when you first read the advert, and now you're about to be put on the spot.

At some point, perhaps at the end of the interview, Chair might ask, *'Are you a genuine candidate for this job, able to accept it if offered*?' That's not such a daft question. It's based on past experience of candidates who've turned jobs down after they were offered.

If you're successful, you may well have to accept the job there and then. If you say, *'Can I think about it?'* they might just agree, especially if they're short of applicants, but there's a serious risk that they'll pass on to another candidate, not only because the panel want things sewn up but because your doubts damage their confidence. If you phone up tomorrow to withdraw, they're back to square one.

So, if your doubts are serious, don't hesitate, or be embarrassed, to withdraw at any point. Your frankness will be appreciated and you'll be doing the other candidates a favour.

Taking stuff in

Some advisers say you can/should have an aide memoir notebook or clipboard with main points on it, and that you should feel free to jot down notes during the interview. That way you don't lose track of a question or you can remember to return to it at the end. There seems no reason why not. It's not an exam or a 'Paxman' grilling after all. But every interview panel is different and their reactions will vary.

You can take your portfolio into the interview with you but make sure it's carefully prepared so you can get at what you want easily, without fumbling. Rehearse this in mock scenarios with friends. Introduce your portfolio as soon as you sit down because if you don't, the panel will remain curious about it. Say something like:

'I've brought some items in my portfolio and I'd like to use them to illustrate some of my points if you don't mind.' They can hardly refuse, and they should be impressed.

When you're asked about planning, for example, produce one of your planning documents, pass it around and speak about it. Try to use everything that's in your portfolio – you'll have been very focused in choosing the items.

Game on

Someone will fetch you, open the door and usher you in. From the moment the door opens and your usher pointedly stands aside to let the panel take a look at you in your glory, the interview is underway.

- Wait to be asked to sit down. If no one says anything, say *'Shall I sit here?'*
- Don't walk to the table and shake hands
- Sit well – straight but not rigid, head up, eyes moving round the panel. Keep your hands under control; lightly clasped is best. Feet on the ground, perhaps with ankles crossed, is a good, comfortable position. Legs uncrossed is best, but at any rate don't keep crossing and uncrossing
- They'll be fiddling with papers and perhaps muttering; keep calm
- When the Chair looks up and smiles, smile back
- When the Chair greets you, reply politely and look alert

The game is now well and truly on.

Format

Interviews are structured to ensure each candidate has an equal chance. The panel will include the head and a colleague as a minimum; the head, senior colleagues, one or more governors and an LEA adviser as a maximum. They will have drawn up a list of questions which are shared out around the panel. This can mean:

- Questions can sound stilted and formal
- Questions might be asked by panel members who know little about the subject
- Some questions seem awkwardly placed in relation to others – a mental leap is required that can throw you
- Some questions, because framed by a committee, are difficult to understand

The important questions are usually the follow-ups in which other panel members pick up on your answers to the structured questions. The head (or department head) and adviser are usually to the fore in follow-up questions and discussion.

Remember, keep calm and keep control: think before you speak and don't be afraid to ask for clarification.

The governors

In a UK state school the voting members of your interview panel – so the ones who ultimately count – are the governors.

New and inexperienced teachers don't always understand this because recruitment for junior posts is often delegated to the school. But in some schools governors won't hesitate to reject the advice of the head and local authority. They may well argue that their long-term concern for the school extends further than the career of one head, and that the local authority's county- or city-wide priorities may not coincide with theirs. So:

- Never in attitude or word appear to dismiss the views of a governor
- Do not play only to the headteacher
- Do not assume that a governor who says little or nothing is not influential
- Do make every effort to understand the governors' vision for their school

It's a conversation

A job interview is ideally a professional conversation not an interrogation. That means you're expected to keep some control. Feel free to use such conversational ploys as:

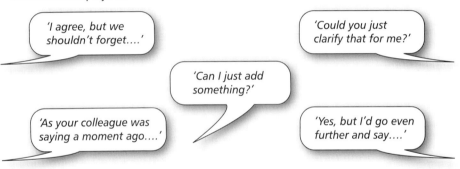

'I agree, but we shouldn't forget....'

'Could you just clarify that for me?'

'Can I just add something?'

'As your colleague was saying a moment ago....'

'Yes, but I'd go even further and say....'

But all the time, be very sensitive to the reactions. You want to see nods and smiles from most of the panel. Don't be worried if the head and/or the local authority adviser keep deadpan faces. Quite often they do this deliberately.

Typical questions

Everything depends on what the job is. Here's just a flavour of the conventions and style:

> 'Did you enjoy your visit to our school?'

Don't just say yes. Make at least one point about the pleasant nature of the children and the excellent atmosphere in the classrooms.

> 'Why did you apply for this job?'

Be positive. For example, you've gathered valuable experience in a good school, and you're ready to take on more responsibility.

> 'Describe a lesson you've taught that you thought went particularly well.'

Smile at what should be a pleasant memory. Mention the children. But above all pin down what the children actually learned and how you know that.

A tricky question

A panel will commonly ask, 'What would you say is your main weakness?'

Frame the answer with the job in mind. A couple of good responses:

Inexperienced teacher:
'There have been times when I should have been a bit quicker to ask colleagues for advice.'
But be ready with an example.

Senior management:
'I've tended to push on, taking insufficient notice of people with genuine reservations. I recognise that now, and I'm constantly telling myself to be more of a listener.'

Beware of 'false weaknesses' such as,
'If I have a weakness it is that I'm a perfectionist ......'

On the other hand,
don't admit to serious problems,
'I'm very indecisive ....'

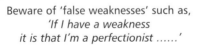

More tricky questions

'Do you enjoy a challenge?'

'Yes, but a genuine challenge is inevitably scary at first, then enjoyable as you realise you can do it. Experience makes you quicker at moving from fear to confidence.'

(For the icing on the cake, have an example ready from your present job.)

'Are you ever angry with your pupils?'

'Yes. An effective teacher is emotionally engaged at every level. But it's the teacher's job to keep emotions under control, and to judge precisely how much to show. So controlled anger can sometimes be used to show disapproval of the actions of a child who is still respected.'

'Where will you be in five years?'

New teacher: *'I hope to be still teaching, to be carrying some responsibility, to be more confident and professionally more assured and able. I don't know if I'll still be here or whether you'll want me to be, but whichever, I'd like to think I'll be looking back with gratitude at the start I had with you here.'*

'Where will you be in five years?'

Senior teacher: *'If I'm still here, and I may well be, given the importance of this post – no promises, mind! (smile) – then I hope I'll at least be looking seriously for my next upward step. I'll certainly have been preparing myself for it in ways that will benefit the school as well as my own development.'*

Common interview mistakes

Talking too much is the most common fault in interviews. Many candidates go into the room mentally repeating, *'I must not talk too much.'* Then they do exactly that.

The solution is to pause to order your thoughts before answering. No one will mind your doing this.

You can say (and it'll get nods and smiles), *'There's so much to say about this, it's difficult to know where to start. So I'll just pick on what I think is one of the key issues ....'*

Then make two or three firm points, mentally count them off and shut up.

You can always say, *'There's more to say if you need it, but I'll stop there for now.'*

Watch for signs that you've gone on too long: panel members exchanging glances or sorting papers to prepare for the next question. Equally, don't talk too little. The monosyllabic and glum candidate isn't going to get the job.

Common interview mistakes

Other common faults include:

Criticising your present school. Interviewers think it says more about you than about the people you're criticising. Instead, speak about your present job as a firm basis from which you're going to move on to higher things.

Dwelling on how important you are to your present school. Instead, describe how your experience is going to help in the job you're being interviewed for.

Over-confidence from someone applying for a junior position. As a new teacher you're in a good position to say, *'I don't know but I'm very willing to learn.'* An open, willing, enthusiastic style is very acceptable to a headteacher. And if you do have some expertise, offer it modestly: *'I specialised in ICT at university, but I'd need to spend some time learning how my knowledge can support the curriculum.'*

No evidence of having found out about the school or the job. Asking, *'You do have a sixth form don't you?'* or *'Is that a council estate opposite?* doesn't demonstrate an appropriate level of interest. It shows you've done no homework.

More interview mistakes

- Any indication that you're not going to stay very long
- Any indication that you're shopping around without much of a plan
- Offering excuses instead of just being honest about lack of experience or knowledge
- Showing intolerance or prejudice
- Cynicism as opposed to considered opinion (about Government/Ofsted initiatives and so on)
- Mentioning influential friends. (Instantly fatal to your chances)

A good answer

A good answer is neither too long nor too short. Try thinking of three-part answers:

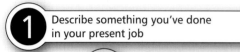

1 Describe something you've done in your present job

2 Say what you learned from the experience

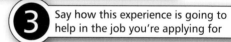

3 Say how this experience is going to help in the job you're applying for

Example question

'Could you tell us about a project or initiative in your present job that you're especially proud of?'

Example answer

'My head of department asked me to organise the science department's contribution to the school open evening. I decided to have a lot of activity going on: experiments happening in all the labs, things for young children to see and do and for mums and dads to have a go at. I involved boys and girls from Y9 mostly, and it really captured their enthusiasm. They enjoyed the responsibility and the feeling of importance as they showed people around. I have this lovely memory of one particularly notorious lad helping an elderly lady to look into a microscope and enjoying a laugh with her.

It taught me the value of giving children responsibility, building their confidence. I saw children of all abilities working together, supporting each other. I learned that parents are genuinely interested in school, and have good questions and ideas to offer. And I think all of that would stand me in good stead as a head of department here.

I know you're interested in developing personalised learning, and in motivating children to take responsibility and in building home-school links. That was just one project, but it taught me a lot, and it was a good example of what I hope is my whole approach to the job.'

You don't know the answer

You're asked a question and your mind is a total blank; you've no idea what to say. That's always likely to happen, so don't be taken by surprise. Here's the plan.

Say, *'I'm sorry, could you just repeat that for me?'* This gives you thinking time, and may actually jiggle your mind into action.

If there's a word or an acronym or abbreviation you don't understand, don't be afraid to ask what it means. That's better than guessing wrong.

If you're still stuck, say, *'Could you just clarify the question a bit for me please?'* Then listen for bits that you do understand and latch on to them, eg *'I'm not familiar with that particular aspect of XXXX, but I do have some firm views about XXXX in general.'* Then wait and see if they ask you to go on.

Navigating a question you can't answer

Headteacher: *'We use AD for behaviour at this school. Have you any views about that?'*

You: *'Could you just repeat that please? AD?'*

Headteacher: *'Assertive Discipline. How do you feel about using that?'*

You: *'Sorry, that's a system of behaviour management is it? Yes? I have to say I've no experience at all of that. I do have definite views about managing classroom behaviour though, and if you wouldn't mind briefly explaining Assertive Discipline I'll answer your question, as well as I feel able.'*

The head used the initials deliberately, and naughtily, to see if you recognised them. You didn't, even though AD has been around a long time, but you didn't bluff or waffle, and you've now got through the rapids in good order.

Navigating a question you can't answer

Poor questions – incoherent, badly phrased, or too broad in scope – are more difficult to answer than good ones. Take a moment to mentally frame a better question, then answer that one, eg:

'Do you think literacy hours are productive in terms of behaviour?'

'What you're asking is whether the literacy hour turns some children off and causes them to behave badly. Well, in my opinion ....'

'What's your opinion of special educational needs?'

'Should all children with SEN be in mainstream schools? Well, in my experience ....'

Be confident and fluent. Smile at the questioner, inviting a return smile or nod. Don't leave a gap after your reframing of the question and don't worry: the panel will invariably go with you.

Talk about children

A surprising number of job candidates never mention children.

In your examples, mention work with children. Give examples, by name. Smile when you do so – just **show that you like children and enjoy being with them**.

Anything you want to ask us?

At the end you'll be invited to add or ask anything. **This isn't a trick.** If you have no questions, say so confidently with a smile:

> *'I had an excellent tour of the school and I think we covered most of the immediate questions then.'*

> *'I feel I've had a good introduction to the post and the school, thank you.'*

Or if you feel relaxed:*'I'm sure I'll think of lots of questions when I get outside, but nothing comes to mind just now.'* That will usually produce the response, *'Well, don't hesitate to phone if you want to clear anything up,'* and a very grateful and gracious response from you, *'That's very kind, thank you very much.'*

The 'add anything?' question is your opportunity to reinforce very briefly a key point you made earlier, or to mention something important that you think's been missed.

Interview by the students

The practice of asking interview candidates to meet with, or be interviewed by, a group of students is increasing in both primary and secondary. You may meet a chosen group, perhaps the school council. Remember these points:

- The questions might be quite stilted, having been carefully discussed (perhaps with help from a teacher) in advance. For example, *'What, is your opinion about homework?'* Or *'Do you think exams are important?'*
- The children probably lack experience in following up prepared questions
- They will all, without fail, understand the importance of what they're doing and take it very seriously
- They'll give feedback to the panel, but sometimes very indirectly to their own teacher first, then from the teacher to a panel member
- The detail of the feedback is often less important than just one flash of valuable insight

Dealing with the students' interview

The word that children use most often of teachers they like is 'kind'. So if you're that sort of person, make sure it comes across. Think also about a sense of humour – children like that, too – and fairness. In a short interview that really means:

- Smiling, making eye contact, speaking gently and without condescension
- Listening carefully to each individual, again with eye contact
- Making a point of drawing in quiet children, showing you want to include everyone
- Making it a conversation. Ask them what they like about their school, for instance, but don't wait for follow up questions that don't come
- Making firm statements about bullying, working hard, helping everyone to do their best

Teaching a lesson

Teaching a lesson as part of the interview process puts you in an unnatural and unnerving position. Psych yourself up to be confident, in charge and steady under fire. Make the class see that you're the teacher and you're going to teach them.

- **Show confidence** – don't wring your hands/blink nervously/keep saying 'sorry'
- **Show enthusiasm** – but don't force it, because it'll be obvious
- **Demonstrate subject knowledge** – be on top of the subject content of the lesson, ready for pupils' questions
- **Show that you like the children** – observers want to see some warmth, kind words, smiles, the twinkle that shows you just like being with young people
- **Engage the students by name** – have sticky labels and get pupils to write their own name tags. Use the names, spread questions around, move among the students. Praise by name, admonish by name if necessary
- **Give praise** – but relate it to the work. Not just, *'Well done Emma!'* but *'That's a good answer Emma, you made the right connection between ......'*

Teaching a lesson

Keep a careful watch on the time. You want your lesson to end tidily so leave enough time for the plenary; it's your opportunity to show what the class has learned.

If you gave work out, collect it in, promise to mark it, and be sure that you do. And finally, leave the room as you found it, showing courtesy to the teacher who has to follow you.

If the lesson goes wrong and you 'lose' the children because, eg it's too hard/easy for them, there are disruptive pupils or the equipment doesn't work, don't despair.

All your observers will be interested in is how you deal with the problem. If you pull things back and move to a successful conclusion, you will gain considerable credit.

Lesson post-mortem

You'll be asked, perhaps in the interview, perhaps immediately after the lesson, how the lesson went.

- Be honest. If they think you can't recognise your mistakes, you won't get the job
- Be precise. Categorise parts of the lesson as good, satisfactory or unsatisfactory, with a clear account of what lies behind your judgement
- Remember that what matters is whether the children learned what you set out to teach them

Most importantly, show clearly, with specific examples, that you know how you could have done better.

A presentation to the panel

Depending on the post you're applying for and the school's preference, you may be asked – in addition to or instead of teaching a lesson – to give a presentation to the interview panel, or sometimes to a wider group of staff and governors which will include the interview panel.

Find out in advance where you're going to give the presentation, who will be present and whether or not you're expected to use ICT. Ask to see the room, if possible, and to see and handle any equipment you might need to use in advance. If you're relying on any kind of overhead slides, check the lighting to ensure they will be visible.

A presentation to the panel

You will usually be asked to present on a subject chosen from a given list. The range of possible topics is wide and will obviously vary according to the post you are applying for. Some actual examples include: building an effective team; working with other agencies in an extended school; involving parents in their children's learning; encouraging creativity in the classroom.

Study the list well and choose your topic carefully, not just on the basis of your knowledge, but also on how well it plays to your presenting strength, eg:

* Explaining statistical data
* Describing case studies of children
* Describing examples of teaching and learning
* Describing case studies of leadership or management issues

The purpose of the presentation

The panel will view the presentation as an opportunity to see you in a different light from that of the interview, but different individuals may be looking for different things. Think of it as an opportunity to show:

- Good work you've done in the classroom
- Enthusiasm for drawing good work from children
- Knowledge of your subject as it's applied in class
- You can give clear and interesting explanations to an audience
- You have some understanding of what lies ahead in the job you're applying for
- You have early ideas about how to use your experience in the new job

The classic mistake is to lose your sense of proportion and spend too much time thinking about and working on the visual aids. This presentation is different from a 'real world' presentation where most of the observers' attention is on the topic. Though your approach to the topic is important, the focus here is on you as a person and speaker. Prepare accordingly: keep it simple, clear, concise.

A simple, clear, concise presentation

Simple Extract one or two key points from the offered topic, eg:

> *'The most important part of a behaviour management policy is that it should have at least as much emphasis on praise and reward as on punishment and sanction. So I'm going to give you my views on and experience of giving rewards and praise in the classroom.'*

Clear Don't use jargon. You may have an audience with a majority of non-teachers. Have a clear beginning, middle and end. The old adage, *'Tell them what you're going to say, say it, tell them what you said'* is more pertinent than you think.

Concise Have a clear mental view of what the final two sentences will be. Don't ramble on beyond them or be dragged lamely onwards by the impassive faces of the listeners.

Keep in touch with the job

In your presentation don't just describe what you're doing in the current job. Relate it to the job you're applying for. As with interview questions, think of three parts, whatever the topic:

1 Briefly describe how you're tackling it in your present job.

2 Explain what you've learned or are learning along the way.

3 Say how you hope your learning can be applied and extended in the job you're applying for.

Time proportions in a ten-minute talk should be about three, three and four minutes respectively.

Presentation techniques

Key points:

- You don't have to use presentation software (unless it's specified) There is a phenomenon known as 'death by PowerPoint®'
- Using presentation technology as you talk (even simple OHP) is an acquired skill, so practise before the day
- If you do use slides of any kind, use them sparingly
- Keep on-screen text brief and graphics simple and clear
- Resist the overwhelming urge to keep turning, pointing and talking to the screen
- Don't just read a slide. It must add value to what you're saying
- Don't rely entirely on technology. Prepare for a power cut

Some presentation do's and don't's

Do

✔ Speak with expression. Use prompt cards and look up, especially as you reach the key words

✔ Feel you can move around, but in a planned and purposeful way, signalling a change of direction or emphasis in your argument, for instance

✔ Wear clothes that are comfortable, that you aren't tempted to fiddle with and which won't fall down, ride up, burst open, gape or strangle!

Don't

✘ Over-run. That's a double whammy – it's irritating and shows lack of preparation

✘ Use jargon

✘ Apologise for anything short of being physically sick

✘ Get flustered – be frank about errors or breakdowns and calmly set about correcting them

✘ Persevere too long with failed technology. (If things aren't working, give up and continue unaided. Carry this off well and you'll come out with brownie points)

Rehearse it

Rehearse your talk without any visual aids at all. Make sure you can make it flow all the way through – for all you know you'll have to do it that way.

Rehearse in front of trusted people who will make notes and give you feedback. The tests are simple:

* Could they hear your words clearly?
* Were they attracted or distracted by your facial expressions and gestures?
* Did you exhibit any unconscious faults such as a nervous cough, many *'ums'* and *'ers'*, vocal tics such as, *'What I'm trying to say ......'* *'OK?'* *'The point is.......?'*
* Did you meet their gaze and smile?
* Did you distribute your voice and gaze around the panel?

In-tray exercise

For senior posts, as well as the interview and presentation, you may be asked to complete an in-tray exercise. You will be given either:

Example 1

A description of a number of incidents happening more or less at the same time:

- Irate parent in the entrance hall
- Caretaker reporting heating breakdown
- Ofsted on the phone
- Angry dog in playground

You'll get the tasks described on paper and you'll have, say, 30 minutes to write what you'd do.

Example 2

A tray of papers that refer to the job, with some written tasks based on them.

In both cases the task is largely to do with your ability to keep calm and prioritise.

Example 1

Your first priority should always be the physical safety of the children. So:

1 If there's a dog in the playground, send whichever teachers are available to bring the children in and sit them in the hall. Tell at least one member of staff to make sure the dog is kept outside. Everything else, including the Ofsted phone call, can wait until you're sure this is proceeding successfully.

2 Instruct your secretary to take the name and number of the person calling and advise them you will phone back.

3 Ask your irate parent to take a seat in the waiting area, explaining what's going on and reassuring him/her that you will certainly listen once you have things settled.

4 To your caretaker, *'OK Jack, so the heating's off. We're getting the children in the hall with their coats on anyway. Meanwhile, could you go to the office and talk to the secretary about who we should be contacting'.*

Example 2

Keep an eye on the time, because your aim is to finish the task. Don't just start at the top and work your way down. Go through the whole pile quickly, assessing which tasks will eat up most time. You may have a set of documents such as these:

- A spreadsheet showing how the school budget is going
- The PANDA (performance and assessment report)
- A letter of complaint from a parent
- A request for a reference

The panel wants a calm and competent response. Nobody expects you to have the detailed background knowledge. Just write in a way that indicates your thinking. With sets of figures, do enough to show that you understand what they're saying in general terms. (Improvement in English, decline in maths and so on.)

As a general rule, the tasks should be well within your competence, so if you're applying for a senior leadership role, make sure in advance that you know how to read the PANDA, have a good idea what a school budget document looks like and know how a parent has the right to be addressed by their child's school.

Starting Out and Moving On

 Job Seeking

 Gathering Information

 Writing the Application

 Preparing for Interview

 Interview Day

 The Interview

 It's All Over

It's All Over

At the end of the day

After the last candidate, the panel will discuss all of you and decide who's to be offered the job. They may keep you all waiting at school or they may ring everyone later.

Sometimes a job offer is 'subject to confirmation by the governors' but that should be a formality. Rarely does anything go wrong.

Paperwork follows later, sometimes a long time later. This can be worrying, but it's almost always down to pressure of work in an office somewhere, and there's nothing sinister going on. The contract *will* come. Quite often it's after you've started work.

Salary negotiations

Can you negotiate your salary? The consensus is yes, you can negotiate your salary – politely, and in a spirit of enquiry rather than demand. Nobody will be offended.

- Just wanting more money isn't enough. You need a very good reason – prior relevant experience, for example, with evidence
- Much depends on how badly the school wants you/needs your shortage subject
- You probably won't get much
- Be ready to be disappointed. Many schools have already fixed the salary in the annual budget and in the staffing policy and there's genuinely no leeway

The time to negotiate is probably when you've got the job and the formal offer arrives, although even here there are exceptions. Here's a TES forum story from a newly appointed deputy head:

'When they asked if I had any questions, I queried the salary and said that I was very keen on the post but that the money on offer was a little on the low side. I kept it very polite and respectful. They gave me the job and agreed to increase the money.'

Second thoughts

So, you've accepted the job, shaken hands and left the panel feeling satisfied they've got the right person and can all relax. But you're having second thoughts. Maybe the job's not what you thought. Perhaps the house prices are too high. Should you phone up and say you've changed your mind?

Strictly speaking you can't pull out after accepting. And you should have cleared up all the problems in advance. However, if you do withdraw, you'll get away with it, but you'll leave a bad impression that won't help if you try for anything else in the same neck of the woods. Heads talk to each other. So the general rule is don't do it, and in any case don't do it more than once.

Bad thoughts

Sometimes a candidate accepts a job knowing that they have another interview the next day. They get the second job and then pull out of the first one. It's just possible that you'll get away with this. But whoever gave you a reference may not be so willing another time. And in any case it's dishonest, unethical, unprofessional and unworthy of a person who wants to be a guide and mentor to young people.

> *'If I discovered that someone on my staff had got their job with me on that basis my opinion of them would dive, and it would take a very long time to recover.'*
>
> **Headteacher**

If you have two interview offers, then you have to decide whether to go to the first one or not. If you do, and don't get the job, then you can go to the second one with a clear conscience. If you get the first job, then you must immediately – preferably the same day – phone up and withdraw from the second interview.

Don't despair

Of course you won't always be offered the job. You're fed up – BUT don't despair – you've been seen by influential people. They'll remember if you did well.

Head 1 to Head 2:

'Hi Joan, you know that vacancy you have for a history specialist? Well you might be interested in someone we interviewed yesterday. Didn't quite fit our needs, but a really good person, excellent interview. Shall I shoot the paperwork over to you?... No problem, it's a pleasure.'

This isn't conjecture. It happens.

If you didn't get the job, you'll wonder why. Don't hesitate to ask if you can talk your interview over with someone. It's rare for this to be refused.

Conclusion

Teaching's one of those careers where for many – perhaps most – people the next job is always on the horizon and sometimes a lot closer than that. It's not just the search for promotion that makes it so. There's a whole lot of other factors: love, money, family, restlessness, mid-life angst, moments of madness, all play their part.

That being so, it's hardly surprising that what looks from the outside like a steady and uneventful path through a series of jobs is actually, seen from within, marked by many moments of high drama. Euphoria? Yes, that'll be there, and so will disappointment and despair.

What's true, though, is just how frequently you can meet in our schools personable, diligent and inspirational teachers who have made it through the obstacle course of application and interview and landed the jobs that they were so obviously cut out for. Maybe they didn't get there the first time, or even the second, third, or fourth. In the end, though, if the qualities are real, and the applications are carefully made, sooner or later, that job comes along. Keep the faith.

Further Information

Where to look for teaching jobs

www.academicsltd.co.uk

www.education-jobs.co.uk

www.tes.co.uk

http://education.guardian.co.uk

www.eteach.com

www.doctorjob.com/teaching

www.teachernet.gov.uk/jobs

Background knowledge

www.tda.gov.uk
Training and Development Agency
for Schools

www.teachernet.gov.uk
Government site

www.becta.org.uk
British Educational and Communications
Technology Agency

www.ncsl.org.uk
National College for School Leadership

For subject teachers, especially in secondary, it's vital to keep in touch with subject
associations. The TDA site has a page of links to all of them.

About the author

Gerald Haigh

Over a thirty-five year career Gerald Haigh taught in primary, middle, secondary modern, bilateral, comprehensive and special schools and in further education. For 11 of those years he was head of a middle school. During and after his full-time teaching career he spent some years as an external examiner to two initial teacher education courses.

After leaving full-time teaching, he worked with his local authority as a trainer of school governors and was himself chair of governors of a primary school.

Both as a head and a governor he was continuously involved in teacher, deputy head, and headteacher recruitment, working closely with his LEA to ensure school appointment procedures were effective, fair, and up to date.

Gerald has been a regular contributor to the Times Educational Supplement and other periodicals and publications for many years and has written several books for teachers. He can be contacted on gerald.haigh@btinternet.com

Order Form

Your details

Name _____

Position _____

School _____

Address _____

_____

_____

Telephone _____

Fax _____

E-mail _____

VAT No. (EC only) _____

Your Order Ref _____

Please send me:

		No. copies
Jobs & Interviews	Pocketbook	☐
_____	Pocketbook	☐
_____	Pocketbook	☐
_____	Pocketbook	☐
_____	Pocketbook	☐

Order by Post

Teachers' Pocketbooks

Laurel House, Station Approach
Alresford, Hants. SO24 9JH UK

Order by Phone, Fax or Internet

Telephone: +44 (0)1962 735573
Facsimile: +44 (0)1962 733637
E-mail: sales@teacherspocketbooks.co.uk
Web: www.teacherspocketbooks.co.uk